CPS

for Teens

Classroom activities for teaching
Creative Problem Solving

Patricia A. Elwell, Ph.D.
Edited by Donald J. Treffinger, Ph.D.

Illustrations by Terry Todoroff

©1993
Prufrock Press

ISBN1-882664-07-8

Table of Contents

ACCEPTANCE-FINDING

GETTING YOUR ACT TOGETHER

CREATIVE PROBLEM SOLVING

Introduction

6   This book was written to be used in a classroom situation. Most of the exercises presented here have been field tested in regular classrooms which span the range of the adolescent years. The youngest students to use the book were sixth graders and the oldest were high school seniors. The field testing showed good results at all levels.

The model of Creative Problem Solving followed throughout this book is presented for adults in "Creative Problem Solving; the Basic Course", by Scott G. Isaksen and Donald J. Treffinger (1985).

Although this book is designed to introduce the six steps of Creative Problem Solving in an incremental way, the exercises can be used individually as well. For example, there are exercises for brainstorming and for developing an understanding of the use of criteria which would have application outside a formal introduction to CPS.

After the students have developed some facility in using the CPS techniques, the teacher could easily go back to some of the earlier exercises and use the material developed as a basis for further class work.

Each exercise offers an opportunity to widen the students options in a non-judgmental fashion and then to narrow the options again using criteria developed by the student. Initially, students need help in feeling comfortable with this aspect. This accordian rhythm to the exercises is called the divergent and convergent parts of an exercise.

The book provides a set of suggestions for the teacher and then presents an activity which is designed for a 42 minute class period. Purchase of the book carries with it permission to duplicate the exercises for your classroom. Pages are marked, "... Reproduced with permission".

A computer program for the Apple computer is available. The disc has a program using a weighted matrix for solution finding and a practice program for brainstorming. This disc is available from the author at P.O. Box 417, Medfield, MA 02052.

A PROBLEM IS . . .

- trouble

- an obstacle to overcome in order to achieve some desired end

- a situation where you can't figure something out

- something that has to be worked out

- any complication that stops or delays your progress on the way to completing your goal

- a pain in the (!*#'$)

- something that you have to solve. . . like being locked out of the house without a key

- when there's something bugging you and you can't or don't know how to fix it

A CHALLENGE IS . . .

- a dare

- some difficulty

- when you have to think about something

General Introduction to the Student

8　Let's assume that you have never heard anything about Creative Problem Solving (CPS). If you have, that's ok, you're ahead of the game.

CPS is a new way of getting what you want. It's different from many of the problem solving methods that have been around. This is a game where crazy counts. Have you ever been told by some adult that what you are thinking is silly or crazy and to forget it? That won't happen in CPS. Sometimes you have to go west to find east.

Thinking of CPS as a game can be helpful. In this game of solving problems there are two important phases. The first phase is the divergent phase where you can let your imagination have the trip of your life. In the first phase you don't judge the ideas..wild, silly, crazy, new, different are what the game calls for....that's diverging...getting a wide set of choices.

In the second phase of this game, you narrow your choices to your best efforts, and ideas. To do that you will have to use your judgment..that's called," converging".

People who have used CPS know what makes it work best. They have even written down some of the rules for CPS. Here are those rules:

For effective divergent thinking:
1. Don't judge the ideas.
2. Look for lots of ideas.
3. Accept all ideas.
4. Make yourself "stretch" for ideas.
5. Take time to let ideas "simmer".
6. Join ideas together -"be a hitchhiker".

For effective convergent thinking:
1. Be deliberate.
2. Be explicit.
3. Avoid going to the next step too soon.
4. Don't avoid the tough issues.
5. Develop "affirmative judgment".
6. Don't lose sight of your goals.

On the page that follows, you will find a summary outline of the six steps in Creative Problem Solving.

CREATIVE PROBLEM SOLVING

Three Main Components and Six Specific Stages

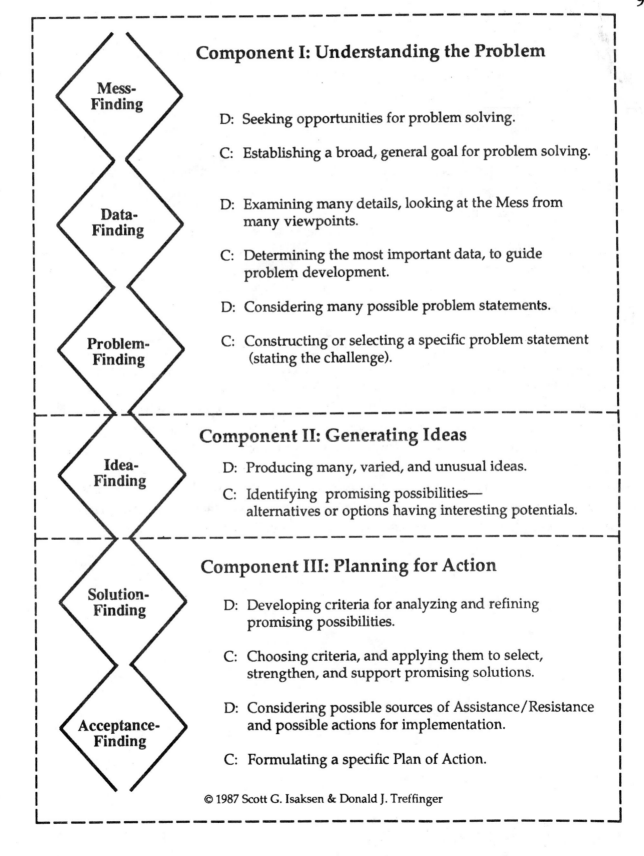

Component I: Understanding the Problem

Mess-Finding

D: Seeking opportunities for problem solving.

C: Establishing a broad, general goal for problem solving.

Data-Finding

D: Examining many details, looking at the Mess from many viewpoints.

C: Determining the most important data, to guide problem development.

Problem-Finding

D: Considering many possible problem statements.

C: Constructing or selecting a specific problem statement (stating the challenge).

Component II: Generating Ideas

Idea-Finding

D: Producing many, varied, and unusual ideas.

C: Identifying promising possibilities— alternatives or options having interesting potentials.

Component III: Planning for Action

Solution-Finding

D: Developing criteria for analyzing and refining promising possibilities.

C: Choosing criteria, and applying them to select, strengthen, and support promising solutions.

Acceptance-Finding

D: Considering possible sources of Assistance/Resistance and possible actions for implementation.

C: Formulating a specific Plan of Action.

© 1987 Scott G. Isaksen & Donald J. Treffinger

Introduction to Getting-Set

Brainstorming is a technique which is used to stimulate a lot of ideas in a short period of time. Brainstorming is used in each of the six steps of Creative Problem Solving. How it applies to each step varies. This first chapter introduces brainstorming as a technique separate from the total CPS process in order to give students a chance to get comfortable with the technique apart from the whole problem solving experience.

In brainstorming an effort is made to go for quantity. One reason for this is that expressing a lot of ideas results in getting out all the usual responses out, as well as the habitual responses. The ideas that have been already tried are aired and part of what happens in brainstorming is a kind of purge. After that, the more unusual, the more imaginative, and the creative ideas have a chance to surface.

In brainstorming it is important to avoid critical comments about the ideas that are offered. This is not always easy for teenagers. These initial practice sessions are included to develop the right atmosphere for successful Creative Problem Solving. As often as not, the teenager holds back in offering an idea because of self criticism. Use these exercises to get ideas flowing freely.

Once the students have caught on to the open-ended nature of brainstorming, they come up with some amazing contributions. The actual generating of ideas is often accompanied by general high spirited participation. Speaking one at a time or waiting to be called on, is often not practical and can inhibit the flow of ideas. The leader of the session will need to hit a balance between a very structured situation where the students are quiet and non-participative and the other extreme where the students are so caught up with the activity and are all speaking so quickly that the ideas are getting lost. Some strategies that have worked to catch the ideas include a tape recorder to supplement what is being written on the papers or more than one person to write down the ideas as they come. Using large pages of newsprint has been the best way to save student work.

GETTING SET

In brainstorming, hitchhiking on someone else's ideas is encouraged. Hearing an idea often triggers a slightly different thought in another participant. Combining, building on, or re-arranging or improving an idea is hoped for and encouraged.

As brainstorming progresses, there are periods when ideas lag. Sometimes there is a need to stimulate further ideas. A question can spur new ideas. As well, asking the students to think of substitutions, adaptations, or ways to combine or re-arrange some element in the situation can start another stream of ideas. The simple technique of magnifying some component or of minifying some aspect can call forth new ideas.

This introductory chapter will also provide some practice in converging. Suggestions will be given for introducing the use of criteria to make selections among the ideas given.

Thus, at the end of chapter one, students will have gained some proficiency in two basic skills for Creative Problem Solving, that is, diverging and converging. As well, the students will have begun to put into practice the ground rules for CPS and will be ready to begin to apply these principles to the six steps of Creative Problem Solving.

GETTING SET

12 Activity #1
A Teabag is a Teabag is a Teabag
Suggestions for the Teacher:

If your class has not had much experience with brainstorming, practicing on a topic which isn't part of a problem can be helpful. Students will need practice in holding back negative responses.

Some people like to chart their progress in "fluency" (that is, how many ideas they can generate in a given period of time).

Activity # 1 works best when the objects are in front of the student. Five or six teabags divided among small groups works well. Allow the students to pass the teabag around and then put it where the group can continue to look at it.

The following list can be used for further practice, after Activity #1 is completed.

Alternative uses for:
> rubber bands
> computer paper strips with holes
> bottle caps
> TV dinner trays
> the round circles that come out of a hole punch machine
> old nylon stockings

After the students have completed the list or after you have had general group response, use the exercise to practice using criteria to select among the items listed. For example, say "If your criterion were to be the most marketable idea among teenagers, which of these alternative uses would you choose? If your criterion is the most unusual, which would you choose? If you were to choose the alternative use which would be closest to art which ones would you choose?" As you do this make note of the fact that the yardstick you use makes a difference in your choice.

GETTING SET

Activity #2
What Do You See?
Suggestions for the Teacher:

In this activity students are asked to let their imagination take a trip. What does the picture suggest to them? The teacher will have to decide whether to use the exercise as a group exercise or an individual one. In field-testing a combination worked well. The students were given five minutes to write down all the ideas that popped into their heads. As a class, then, those ideas were shared. The leader asked at the end of the sharing, "Which idea did you hold back because you thought someone would make a negative comment? Which one did you not share because you thought it was too far out or silly?" The students were then asked to add ten more to the list.

During the five minutes of writing, the students were prompted by the following questions:

> What things in nature does this picture remind you of?
> What household pictures come to mind?
> Does the picture suggest something from the world of machines?
> How about thinking of this picture connected to the city?
> What is the craziest interpretation you can think of? Write it down.
> Apply the picture to the world of animals.

This sort of experience for the students will open them up to the endless variety that our imaginations offer. It sometimes happens that students use this exercise to test the teacher. It will be important for the teacher to maintain a non-judgmental attitude.

Converging

At the end of the session, ask the students to look over the ideas given. Ask the following questions:

- If you were making a jokebook out of these responses, which would you pick?

- If you were to use this as an attention getter for an advertisement, which could you use?

- Which ones would get you in trouble with your parents if they knew you said them? (This last one could be used if there are a number of socially unacceptable ideas.)

GETTING SET

Activity #3
Ping Pong Plenty
Suggestions for the Teacher:

14 This is a good exercise for students to broaden their categories of ideas. For example, there are a number of things one could do with ping pong balls if they are seen as building materials. However, if all the ideas are simply in that category, E. Paul Torrance would say more flexibility is called for. Aim for a number of different sorts of categories, asking the students to consciously change the verbs to stimulate new ideas.

Bob Eberle suggested in his book, *SCAMPER*, that making use of the acronym **SCAMPER** is another idea stimulating technique.

Substitute	What could the ping pong balls become substitutes for?
Combine	What could you do with ping pong balls combined? What could you combine the ping pong balls with to come up with a new idea?
Add	If you added something to the ping pong balls what would you come up with?
Magnify	If you used all the ping pong balls at once in one way, what could you do with them?
Put to Other Uses	Think of some totally new use for ping pong balls.
Eliminate	If you removed part of the ping pong ball or used only part, what could you do with it?
Reverse	What would happen if you reversed the shape in some way?

In a brainstorming session, the use of the word SCAMPER will be useful throughout the book. Use this exercise to introduce how those words can stimulate new ways of getting ideas.

Before the session begins put the word SCAMPER on the board or prepare a handout. Then give the students time to apply the SCAMPER techniques to the ping pong activity.

To introduce some common criteria in converging, ask the students which uses involve the least amount of additional expense? Which ideas for use stand the best chance of increasing their supply of money? Which ideas for use are related to beauty and art uses? Which uses involve no safety hazards at all? Which uses sound like they would be the most fun for teenagers?

GETTING SET

Activity #1
A TEABAG IS A TEABAG IS A TEABAG

You have just been given a teabag. If you weren't going to use it to make a cup of tea, what could you use it for?

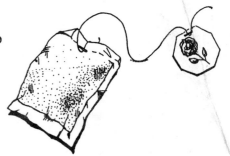

After each question, write down the ideas that pop into your head. Don't judge the ideas or reject them because you may think they are silly.

1. What uses does the smell suggest?

   _____

2. Feel the teabag and write down some ideas.

   _____

3. If you took something away, what could you then do?

   _____

4. How could you re-arrange the parts to create a new use?

   _____

5. If you substituted something, what could you do?

   _____

6. Combine the teabag with something else. What could you use it for?

   _____

7. Think of the teabag in a new context, what could it be used for?

   _____

8. What if you had a thousand teabags, what could you do then?

   _____

9. What could the teabag be a miniature for?

   _____

GETTING SET

Activity #2
WHAT DO YOU SEE?

16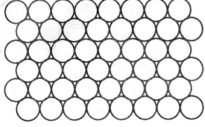

Here's your chance to let your imagination take a trip. You will have five minutes to write down all the ideas that this picture suggests to you. As you write, your teacher will make some comments to trigger associations. Write down the ideas that come to mind. We'll judge the ideas later.

_____
_____
_____
_____
_____
_____
_____
_____
_____
_____
_____
_____
_____
_____
_____
_____
_____
_____
_____
_____
_____
_____

GETTING SET

Activity #3

PING PONG PLENTY

You are visited by an aunt and uncle who own a hardware store which is changing their stock. They bring you a huge box of ping pong balls. There are about 2,000 of them. What could you do with them? In What Ways Might You use the ping pong balls?

_____

_____

_____

_____

_____

_____

_____

_____

_____

_____

_____

_____

_____

_____

_____

_____

_____

_____

_____

_____

_____

GETTING SET

Introduction to Mess-Finding

18   For many people, awareness that a problem has entered their life is a matter of what our colleague Roger Firestien calls a BGO (Blinding Glimpse of the Obvious). Something has happened to upset your plans, or something has gone wrong. It isn't that Creative Problem Solving is meant to be used for every kind of problem. If you are driving along and have a flat tire, you either get the spare out and replace the flat, or call a gas station for help. It would only be special circumstances which would bring CPS into the picture. The classic story is the one about the long distance truck which was fully loaded and came to an overpass. The driver had to stop because the truck was too tall. There was only one road, a single lane for each line of traffic. The traffic in back of the truck quickly formed a long line and people were on the verge of getting impatient. What to do? The driver could, of course, turn around and retrace his way going many miles out of the way. CPS techniques uncovered a novel approach to this problem: let some air out of the tires to lower the top of the truck and thus solve the problem.

In that story, the problem was apparent and the need for solution intense. A lot of our problems are like that. CPS often comes into the picture after a few tries at solving the problem have failed. On the other hand some of the messes in our life have been there for a while and are more nearly described as challenges for improvement or opportunities for growth. CPS can have application there too. You can use CPS whenever you need some fresh new ideas, and a plan for using them.

In the first part of this book, in Mess-Finding, there are a series of classroom activities designed to help you identify some "messes" which would be appropriate for Creative Problem Solving.

In real life, the Mess-Finding stage often comes with its own method of announcement: The report card comes and you have more than half your grades below passing. Your father or mother remarries and you suddenly have to share your room with someone with very different tastes. Opportunities simply present themselves, you may also discover, however, that sometimes it will even help to go "looking for problems" to solve by finding great new opportunities to put your creativity to work!

MESS-FINDING

BEFORE YOU START: Make photocopies of the Mess-Finding Activities #1 through 5 (pages 23 - 29) for each student. Distribute the activity sheets singly, as you become ready to use them.

Activity #1
Creative Challenge Goulash
Suggestions for the Teacher:

The purpose of this activity is to loosen up the student in regard to problems and challenges that can be used with this book. To learn Creative Problem Solving with non-real problems is the quickest way to kill your efforts. So, at the outset be prepared for some follow through as the course progresses.

In Activity #1, the goal is to trigger new combinations by word association. The format given is only one way to use the word lists. Another way to use it, would be to create a morphological chart using the three sets of words. This would require advance preparation by the teacher. First, the lists would be put on a large chart in separate moveable columns. Next, a cover would be made such that only one word from each column would show. Finally, the students would be asked to provide the ideas for challenges as the columns of words are randomly changed. The ideas that the students come up with should be saved for later use, just as in the exercise which is provided. One difference between the two methods of use is that the exercise as given is an individual exercise. The chart method would be a group activity. Both methods could be used as separate class activities.

Activity #2:
Challenges for the 21st Century
Suggestions for the Teacher:

Divide the class into small groups on the basis of topic. Appoint or get a volunteer from each group to write down the ideas that the group comes up with.

Topic Areas:
>   Politics/World Government/Aggression
>   Religion
>   Energy/Resources/Environment
>   Relations with People
>   Food/Clothing/Shelter
>   Business/Industry/Earning a Living

Add other areas to this list if desired.

MESS-FINDING

Procedure:

1) Brainstorm* all the problems/challenges that come to mind for your topic area. (5-10 minutes)

2) Keeping your groups the same, exchange problem areas and lists. Brainstorm that groups' topic area for 3-5 minutes. Return lists to original group.

3) The teacher then makes the following suggestions. After each question your group should try to increase their list.

   Stretching Your List

   a) Add the problems in your topic area that are based on the need to eliminate something undesirable.
   b) Add to your list those problems that center on the need to add something that's important, needed or desired.
   c) What problems are mainly based on a need to substitute one thing for another..add it to your list.
   d) Think of a problem or challenge that involves a wish or desire to adapt to new conditions, or the need to put something to another use..increase your list.
   e) Now think of all the problem areas, what problems/challenges are suggested by thinking of them in combination?

4) Still in your groups, narrow the list down to the one challenge your group wants to do something about. Vote for your choice, each person in the group gets one vote. Before you vote, ask yourself, is this really my problem? Can I actually do anything at all about it? You won't be working on getting ideas for your choice if this is a single class period exercise, but your choice could be used later in the course, so choose a challenge where you are really willing to put new ideas to the test.

   The group recorder should circle the idea chosen and the entire list should be saved.

5) The class period could end with the group recorder reading the chosen challenge.

*If your students are not familiar with brainstorming, turn to the 1st exercise for "Idea-Finding" and refer to the Guidelines for Brainstorming.

MESS-FINDING

6) Arrange for some means of sharing these ideas. They could be posted on a bulletin board, or duplicated so each student gets a total list. Let the students participate in this. In any event, keep a copy of these challenges. Your students may choose to use some of the ideas later in the book. Some teachers keep an ongoing Creative Problem Solving Bulletin Board in one part of the room to post information and class work as the exercises are used.

Activity #3
Personal Inventory Exercise
Suggestions for the Teacher:

This exercise can serve as practice in brainstorming. For example, before the students begin, use 5 to 10 minutes in a brainstorming session on the topic of "In What Ways Might a shy person become less shy." If you know your class is full of extroverts, use another topic, such as, "In What Ways Might I improve my skills as a basketball player" or "In What Ways Might I improve my grades."

This sort of exercise could be used to introduce Scamper. Give the students a copy of the Scamper check list to assist them. If students already know the list ask them to consciously use it now.

Since this exercise is largely done alone, you might want to make use of some "mind joggers" as the students are working.

Mind Jogging Suggestions:

1) Think of three people whom you really admire. What qualities do you admire most? Does that suggest something for your own list of ways you could improve?

2) Maybe there's some aspect to your life that you would really like to eliminate . . . maybe that would be an improvement.

3) Is there some aspect to your personality that is a problem, which if you directed it differently might become an improvement? For example, if people tell you you're too rough, maybe you should think of getting into something where strength is an asset.

Note: As with the other introductory exercises - Later in the course students may wish to use some part of this exercise as one of their problem solving projects.

MESS-FINDING

Activity #4

Regional News
Suggestions for the Teacher:

This activity will provide the opportunity to identify possible areas for problem solving. Since it is introspective, it is best done as an individual activity. The session could end with sharing the topic chosen for the newspaper article.

Activity #5

Textbook Improvement
Suggestions for the Teacher:

Students will need a textbook with them for this exercise. Since the goal for almost all school textbooks will be the same, that is, to help the student in the mastery of a subject matter, students may use different books. This exercise would work well in small groups using the same book.

GOALS:

1) For students to realize that just about anything can be improved if the effort is made.

2) Problems don't have to be narrowly defined, but can include something you wish were improved.

3) To put into practice some of the techniques for creative thinking.

Have students read the introduction, then distribute the review sheet.

Follow up Suggestions: Since most major textbook companies have periodic revisions of their textbooks, it is entirely possible that this exercise could have "real life" applications. If any of your students pursues this with a textbook company, please share the information with me.

MESS-FINDING

Activity #1
CREATIVE CHALLENGE GOULASH

INSTRUCTIONS TO THE STUDENT: Word association can trigger new ideas. These three lists are provided to stimulate ideas for challenges (problems to solve). Take a word or two from each list. Combine several or a couple to come up with some challenges. For example: In What Ways Might I do my chores more efficiently to gain more leisure time? In What Ways Might I overcome my disappointment at not being invited to a special party this weekend?

List for Creative Challenge Goulash

school	telephone	difficulty
friends	food	popularity
teachers	looks	performance
family	clothes	fear
neighbors	violence	anxiety
sports	alcohol	distrust
church	drugs	waste
money	cars	inefficient
wishes	T.V.	efficient
hopes	weekends	safety
dreams	overcome	increase
leisure time	improve	decrease
career	comfort	prolong
college	happiness	prevent
chores	disappointment	lack
homework	care	anger
grades	boredom	hate
parties	understanding	disgust
music	misunderstanding	ease
		sublimate

INSTRUCTIONS:

I   Write out four challenges for yourself. More if you can.

II   Write out three challenges that you and someone else might tackle together.

III   Write out one challenge for a friend who might be having trouble thinking of challenges.

IV   Look at the four challenges you write for yourself. Place a check by the most urgent in your life. Re-read part two, the challenges you can tackle with a friend. Mark the one that you would like to do first. Save your list for later in the course.

MESS-FINDING

Activity #2
CHALLENGES FOR THE 21ST CENTURY

24 We live in an age where you don't have to look very far to see things that need to be improved. You don't have to think too hard to come up with a list of problems that exist for our country or the planet. Many people feel that we need all the help we can get. Creative Problem Solving seeks to multiply ideas and solutions because when you have a lot of ideas to choose from, your chances of success increase.

As a warm up exercise to Problem Solving to show that there will be many challenges "out there" waiting for a new generation of problem solvers, complete this exercise.

INSTRUCTIONS: Circle the topic your group is doing.

Politics/World Government/Aggression   Religion

Energy/Resources/Environment   Relations with People

Food/Clothing/Shelter   Business/Industry/Earning a Living:

Give the paper to the person who will be the scribe.

FIRST BRAINSTORMING:

_____

SECOND BRAINSTORMING FROM EXCHANGED LISTS:

_____

THIRD BRAINSTORMING FROM STRETCHING SUGGESTIONS:

_____

CONVERGING-CHOOSING A REAL CHALLENGE:

_____

MESS-FINDING

Activity #3
PERSONAL INVENTORY EXERCISE

Even Robert Redford could profit from this exercise! A personal assessment need not be embarrassing or discouraging. Sometimes, it's just the force of habit that keeps people from recognizing a need for change. This exercise is designed to help you become aware of the possible need for change in your own life. It will also serve as an introduction to the positive approach to Creative Problem Solving...notice the phrase "In What Ways Might I.."

Personal Inventory Checklist

1= no problems, I'm satisfied
5= I hate it, if I had a magic wand this would be on my change list.

Instructions: First, go through the following list and assign a number for your own assessment of each area. Don't take too long. Place a number from 1 to 5 in the assessment box. (About 5 minutes)

Attitude:	___	**Appearance:**	___
towards yourself	___	hair	___
towards money	___	weight	___
possessions	___	clothes	___
towards other people	___	skin	___
		voice	___
Character:	___		
fairness	___	**Health:**	___
honesty	___	physical condition	___
kindness	___	energy level	___
generosity	___	other	___
Habits:	___	**Skills:**	___
work/study	___		
personal	___	**Knowledge:**	___
		awareness of	
Social Aspects/Relationships		world affairs	___
to Other People:	___		
friendships	___	**Grades:**	___
general: are you shy?	___		
family	___		

MESS-FINDING

PERSONAL INVENTORY EXERCISE continued

26 Next, look at the areas where you have fives or fours. If you have no number five or four look at your highest number.

Converging:

Which one is the most urgent? Write the area here. _____

Which one, if I did something about it, would change my life?

Write the area here. _____

What do I most want to improve? Write it here. _____

Summary:

You now have a beginning list of areas to use in Data-Finding. Save this list. Before finishing this exercise, select the area you'd like to start with. Remember that a personal change list can be useful for many years. Think about keeping this list for four years. Think about making a new one each of those years. Wouldn't it be interesting to compare the lists and see how you've changed your life to suit your own interests and needs?

MESS-FINDING

Activity #4
REGIONAL NEWS

You've been asked to write several articles for the school newspaper. The only requirement for the articles is that they be about you and your concerns and interests. To prepare you for this assignment, the editor has sent you the following set of questions to help suggest possible topics. Fill out the editor's questionaire.

Write out a few things that are important to you. _____

_____

What are you curious about? _____

_____

How do you work with other people? _____

_____

Thinking back over the last month, what's been bugging you? _____

_____

What are a few things you do well? _____

_____

List a couple things you'd like to do better. _____

_____

In the last year, is there something you've been trying to avoid doing? _____

_____

When you think of the challenges and opportunities that you could tackle, which ones

come to your mind first. _____

_____

What would your best friend say about how you react to new ideas and situations?

_____

Converging
Go back over what you have written, and put an x by the high priority items in your life. What would you most like to write about if you were going to write an article for the paper?

_____

MESS-FINDING

Activity #5
TEXTBOOK IMPROVEMENT

28   INTRODUCTION: A conservative estimate of hours spent by high school students in a given year reading textbooks is 276 hours. Such a large chunk of time means improvement of textbooks could be a real benefit. The following exercise is designed to help you realize that "problem solving" can mean looking for ways to improve. Try to loosen up your imagination in making your suggestions.

TEXTBOOK REVIEW SHEET

Name of Textbook: _____

Publisher: _____

Address of Publisher: _____

Date of Textbook: _____

Physical Characteristics: (Can be improved by:)

Pages: _____

      Color: _____

      Size: _____

Type: _____

      Size: _____

      Shape: _____

Weight: _____

	Yes	**No** (Are they present?)	**Comments** (Can be improved by...)
Pretests to determine what you know already about the subject.	◯	◯	
Practice exercises	◯	◯	
Written text (content)	◯	◯	
Bibliography of other books on the subject	◯	◯	
Chapter summaries	◯	◯	

MESS-FINDING

TEXTBOOK REVIEW SHEET continued

	Yes	No	Comments (Can be Improved by:)
Index	○	○	
Glossary	○	○	
Pictures	○	○	
Cartoons, humor	○	○	
Italics to mark important sentences	○	○	
Answers - different kinds of activities suggested for different ability levels for those who need extra practice, or for those who would like a challenge.	○	○	
Add things that are not listed here:	○	○	

NOW, you have looked at what exists, stretch your imagination.

What isn't there that could be there to aid your mastery of the subject? Don't let your **usual** idea of textbooks keep you from coming up with a really creative idea. For example, with the increase of mini-computers in the classroom, why not offer a computer program keyed to the textbook chapters that would help in reviewing the materials. Schools could order the program to match their computer when they order the textbook.

What else can you think of: _____

_____

Perhaps something should be left out?

Realizing that students learn more easily where they are genuinely interested in a subject - what suggestions do you have to increase student interest?

MESS-FINDING

Introduction to Data-Finding

What is data? How does finding data fit into Creative Problem Solving?

Data is simply information. Collecting information before you start to solve a problem or tackle a challenge can give you new insights into just what the problem or challenge is. An easy way to understand what Data-Finding is all about is with an illustration.

Suppose someone asked you what your school is like? If you answered by saying that there are grades seven through twelve, that there are 700 students, that girls outnumber the boys, then you have given someone some data about your school. If you say that you hate your school, or that you find the school academically tough, then you have given that person some data about you and how you feel, but not data about your school. Both sorts of data could be very important in problem solving.

The kind of problem or challenge which enters your life makes a difference in how much space in which you have to respond. Some problems don't allow for lengthy data collection, but time-line information is important. The simple question, "How long do I have before I have to act?" can be one of the most important questions to answer. "What happens if I do nothing at all?" can yield important data as well. "What's the worst that can happen?" can give a person perspective on the scope of a given challenge or problem. These questions, and others form part of the effort to get as much information as possible before getting launched into figuring out action ideas. Very often the gathering of data produces a broader slant on how to look at a given problem or challenge. After a period of open inquiry, comes selecting or recognizing what information is most pertinent. This task will vary with the client. In some of these exercises, it will work to simply allow someone to be the client who "owns" the problem. It becomes a "what would you have done?" situation.

DATA-FINDING

BEFORE YOU START: Make photocopies of the Data-Finding Activities #1 through 6 (pages 35 - 43) for each student. Distribute the activity sheets singly, as you become ready to use them.

Activity #1
Computer Dating
Suggestions for the Teacher:

The age of the student will determine how this is used. Some students may want to write a computer program to put something like this into action. On the other hand, younger students may have no interest at all.

The exercise can be used to help students familarize themselves with the mechanics of converging. Have the students notice how many number 10's they put down for an activity. That constitutes converging, without talking about the criteria. One way of getting the student to become aware of the fact that registering preference makes use of criteria, is to ask something like, "Why did you give such and such a 10?"

It is not at all unusual for students to shy away from strong preferences. I've seen students give everything a 5. Recognizing that about themselves can be a new insight. Finding out if they also prefer to spend time with people who likewise have that preference can be a growing experience if the teacher is careful to be non-judgmental..that is, if the teacher is careful not to make the student feel there is something wrong with giving a lot of activities a 5.

Activity #2
Boredom in School
Suggestions for the Teacher:

This activity will give your students an opportunity to deal with a problem that never seems to go away. In using it for CPS, you have a chance to develop an issue that can have real classroom applications. In the field testing of this book, students became very involved and used this topic for actual completion of the other steps of CPS.

One word of advice. Acceptance-Finding will be a very important step in handling this in your school.

DATA-FINDING

Activity #3
College Search
Suggestions for the Teacher:

One of the most common problems for high school students in choosing a college is that they start too late. Many decisions are made quickly, without much information. It is not unrealistic for high school sophomores to begin this task. Getting them to see the benefit this brings is a challenge in itself.

Starting early widens the choice. It is surprising how many high school students don't actually know that if they have high SAT scores they stand a good chance of getting scholarships. If the parents are not wealthy, they have two chances for scholarship money, merit and need. Finding out who has money to give away to meritorious or needy students takes time and effort. To do what is necessary certainly is worth it, if the student wants a college education.

This activity can be done singly, as a whole group, or in small groups. Whether it's done in small groups or alone, be sure to allow time at the end of the class period to go over what's done.

Finish with a master list.

Follow up: You might check with the guidance counselor of the school to see if he or she would welcome a copy of your master list. You may find your students have prepared something which could be used in the school. In any event, copies home to the parents might be helpful.

Converging

Getting the students to get a feel for priorities might be useful in this exercise. After they have gone through the questions, have them go back and decide which questions need to be answered first, second, etc.

Don't leave the converging to chance. Ask the students to decide on the priority for themselves, using whatever scale seems appropriate. The time frame will force the student to be prompt, so using a 1,2,3 scale might work best.

DATA-FINDING

Activity #4
Recycled School
Suggestions for the Teacher:

This exercise had its origin in an actual situation. It can be used in a variety of ways.

Since most every town has an empty building, students could convert this to an authentic challenge.

What to do with an old building provides lots of open-ended possibilities that go beyond Data-Finding, so save the work that is done here for an extra exercise in each of the succeeding chapters.

The exercise can be used individually as well as in small groups or one large group. Since sharing ideas with others stimulates ideas, build on that to get a large number of questions for Data-Finding.

Activity #5
Boycott Blues
Suggestions for the Teacher:

This exercise, like the previous one, had its origin in an actual situation. I included it because the crucial difference between the two situations, namely, the short amount of time available before a decision has to be made, affects what you do with a problem, and the kind of data collection you go through.

This one works well as an individual exercise that is shared at the middle and end. It is clearly a "What would you have done situation?"

Activity #6
The Perilous Porch
Suggestions for the Teacher:

In this problem the following questions are the sort that it would be good for students to think of asking:

> What's already been tried?
> Has anyone else already done this sort of thing?
> Who can I get to assist us in this project?
> What sort of information is available for this kind of project?
> What are our resources for the project?

DATA-FINDING

This exercise builds on the experience of doing the Data-Finding flow charts of the other exercises.

Notice that the converging aspect to this exercise is built into the flow chart. It consists of the student deciding on the best sources of information and deciding what has to be known before the next step can be taken. It is another way of recognizing "what the bottom line" is. Don't leave this step to chance. Be explicit.

This exercise is a good one for small groups. What each group comes up with may vary and end of the session sharing will be important.

In any of the exercises where there is small group work, the teacher needs to take care that one responsible note-taker gets the information recorded. If this is done in a total class exercise, a large newsprint page taped to the blackboard is an easy way to record responses.

If you are using this as the last exercise in data-finding, you might consider having one of your brightest students lead the session. There are many places where able students can function as the facilitator. If you keep yourself alert to that possibility in each of the chapters, by the end of the sessions the students will be closer to doing CPS on their own.

DATA-FINDING

Activity #1
COMPUTER DATING

As a money making project to finance the school yearbook, the staff has launched a computer dating service. They are in the process of getting the data into the memory system of the computer and have distributed surveys to all students. You have just received your copy. Please complete the questionaire. When you are finished you will have gathered together in one place a lot of data about yourself. In addition to being an exercise in Data-Finding, perhaps you have become aware of some things about yourself that you weren't aware of before you took the questionaire.

Computer Dating Survey

Age: _____   Height: _____

Acceptable age range for your date: _____

Sex: (circle)   Male   Female

School Information

Classroom grades: circle one

all A's   A's & B's   all B's   B's & C's   all C's   C's & D's   all D's   failing

Do you want your date to match you in grades?   yes or no

Do you want your date to have better grades than you?   yes or no

Do you want your date to have grades that aren't as good as your grades?   yes or no

School subjects: _____

List at least one subject in school that you like. _____

List your least favorite subject. _____

36   Rank each of these leisure time activities. Giving the activity a 1 means you **dislike** the activity a lot. Giving the activity a 10 means you **like** the activity a lot. Giving the activity a number in-between shows which direction you are leaning for that activity. Giving an x for the activity means you've never tried it.

_____ Go to a movie   _____ Go to a square dance

_____ Go dancing (disco)   _____ Go somewhere to slow dance

_____ Go out to dinner   _____ Go to a rock concert

_____ Get together with friends   _____ Get together with friends
          to make dinner   to listen to music & talk

_____ Go to a classical music concert   _____ Go to a political rally

_____ Go on a hike   _____ Go skiing

_____ Go ice skating   _____ Go swimming

_____ Go to a poetry reading   _____ Go to a play

_____ Go see a musical   _____ Go to a beach

_____ Play a musical instrument   _____ Sing

_____ Play tennis   _____ Play golf

_____ Play baseball/softball   _____ Play volleyball

_____ Go to an auction   _____ Go play video games

_____ Go horseback riding   _____ Play cards

_____ Go dancing (fast dancing)   _____ Go to a mall to shop

_____ Talk on the telephone   _____ Go for a ride in a car

_____ Watch T.V.

DATA-FINDING

Activity #2
BOREDOM IN SCHOOL

One of the "messes" that comes up often enough so as to be almost universal is "being bored with school." After thinking about the problem, Tom decided to do something about it and asked his English teacher to conduct a brainstorming session on "In what ways might I reduce classroom boredom." His classroom teacher had never heard of Creative Problem Solving, but was familiar with brainstorming. She was willing and here's the list the class came up with after just a minute or two:

quit school

doodle

while it's boring imagine interesting things

get someone to start an alternative school that isn't boring

slouch down and read an interesting book under the desk

meditate

get the classroom teacher to make it less boring

figure out why it's boring

have a "dress up" day where anything not indecent can be worn

make the classroom more like a library where you can choose what you want to study or read, and where you can choose when you want to do it in peace and quiet

make a list of how to make school not boring

strike up interesting debates with the teacher which are not on the boring subject at hand

get the teachers to do less talking

have each class include 10 minutes of unscheduled time

have a study hall first period for the "non-morning" people

change the students ideas of what is boring

DATA-FINDING

BOREDOM IN SCHOOL continued

38   Many people mistakenly think that brainstorming is all there is to CPS. This exercise should help demonstrate how brainstorming fits in to CPS, but is only one part of a 6 step procedure. Look back over the list. Notice that a student said "Figure out <u>why</u> it's boring." In CPS finding out all the facts that you can <u>before</u> you start generating ideas for the solution is important. The reason it's important is that you'll be more successful in solving the problem.

Back up one step for this exercise and do some "Data-Gathering." Since boredom in the classroom is a problem just about everyone has faced at one time or other you can do the data gathering without much effort.

Do the following:

1) Think about the worst boring class you've had and ask yourself **why** you were bored. Write down the reasons that come to you.

    _____

2) Think of the classrooms where you aren't bored. **What** does the teacher do to avoid boredom. What do the students do. **What's** the difference? Write down your ideas.

    _____

3) **Who** has been thinking about this problem already, and what ideas do they have?

    _____

4) **Who's** involved in this problem?

    _____

5) **What's** involved in this problem?

    _____

6) **When** is it especially boring?

    _____

7) **Who** else might have information about this?

    _____

8) Write down any new relevant pieces of information that you've thought of.

    _____

9) What new insights does this give you on the problem?

    _____

DATA-FINDING

Activity #2
BOREDOM IN SCHOOL continued

Converging

Now that you have some information about school boredom in front of you, mark the items that are most crucial to this subject.

Look at what you have marked. Can any of these concerns be grouped together?
Write them here.

_____

Are there several things that just "hit" you. Remember those "hits" when you restate the problem.

_____

Which of the things which were listed should have something done about them first?

_____

What other data must you get before you go on to the next step?

_____

This exercise started with "In what ways might I reduce classroom boredom?" You are probably ready to begin putting that in other words. Give at least five new ways to state the problem beginning with "In what ways might I/we..."

_____

_____

_____

_____

_____

DATA-FINDING

COLLEGE SEARCH

40   Finding a college that suits you, that your parents are enthusiastic about, which also fits
your budget, can be a real problem. Fact-Finding well in advance of deadlines for
admission can lessen the strain for everyone. Suppose you plan on some sort of after high
school schooling. What facts would help you make a good choice?

What do I want to know about the school before I decide?

_____

When are the deadlines for this decision?

_____

What do my parents want to know:

_____

Where can I get information about this?

_____

What do I need to know about myself before I decide?

_____

What do I hope to gain from the experience at this school?

_____

Who can I talk to about this?

_____

What is preventing me from going where I really want to go?

_____

Why haven't I already solved this problem?

_____

DATA-FINDING

Activity #4
RECYCLED SCHOOL

You've been asked to serve on a committee made up of two school board members, two community members, and a school administrator. They have asked a high school student to participate because the committee seems genuinely interested in getting a wide variety of opinions. The task for the committee is to draw up suggestions for the school board as to what to do with a school building in the district which will be vacant next year. You want to do a good job on the committee. What kind of information would you like to have? What would be helpful to know in thinking about this building? What other data would you like to have?

This exercise has three parts. It can be completed in small groups. Divide the page in half, left and right.

I   On the left half, list the questions about the building for which you want answers. Don't worry about whether you can get the information. What sorts of things must you know to figure out a use for the building?

II   On the right hand side of the page, list where you can get the answers to the question.

III After you have finished your list, go back over the questions. Circle the items that seem the most important to consider. Look at the things you have circled. Is there a pattern? Is there some theme or strand that runs through most of the questions? What should be considered first? After you have finished this section, you have gone through the divergent part of Data-Finding, and have converged. In real life, the next step would be to get the information you asked for and then to start Problem-Finding.

DATA-FINDING

Activity #5
BOYCOTT BLUES
Who What When Where How

42 In a high school that has 535 students grades 7-12, a student boycott of classes has been called. Students plan to leave their classes and stage a protest outside the school. You are being pressured to join the boycott. In discussing the situation with classmates, 20 out of 30 in your science class plan to participate. It is rumored that a well-liked coach has been fired by the Board of Education. The reasons students have given you for joining the boycott are as follows: One said that the majority are going to boycott and so should you. Another said, if you didn't do it you'd be a weird-o. A third said, "What's the matter, don't you like Coach Sanford?" You decide to do some Data-Finding. What questions would you ask?

Instructions: Here is a Data-Finding flow chart. Start with Column I, then go to Column II. If this were an actual case, the next step would be to go to the sources and get some information, and then move to Problem-Finding.

I	II
What information would you like to have about the "mess"? (list data-finding questions, not evaluative or creative ones.) Don't worry about whether you can get the information. If you want it, ask the question. Aim for at least 15 questions. Ask yourself what the essence of the mess is. What do I have to know before I can go on?	Where can you get answers to the questions you circled in I. List all the sources you can think of. Circle what you think might be your best source.

DATA-FINDING

Activity #6
THE PERILOUS PORCH

Your little brother came up to you yesterday with a drawing for a porch to his tree hut. He wanted you to help build it. You'd like to help him build it, but he didn't give you enough information to get going. He had a sketch of what he wanted.

Here it is: He said he wanted a porch "most of the way around the tree."

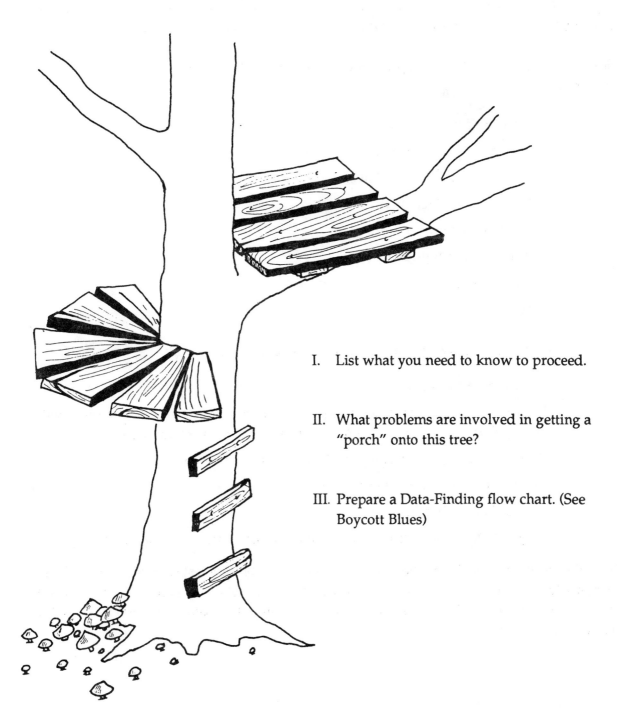

I.   List what you need to know to proceed.

II. What problems are involved in getting a "porch" onto this tree?

III. Prepare a Data-Finding flow chart. (See Boycott Blues)

DATA-FINDING

Introduction to Problem-Finding

44 In this part of Creative Problem Solving the goal is to open up how the problem is looked at as widely as possible and then to select one IWWMI statement which captures the central core of the problem.

It's important to remember that some of the work done in Problem-Finding will uncover aspects to a problem that will be worked on at another time. When the selection is made as to what will get the attention for now, it doesn't eliminate the other possibilities for a later time.

Some of the questions that are especially useful to answer in the divergent part of Problem-Finding are:

> Why is this important to me?
>
> What do I hope to accomplish, or gain?
>
> Why is this a problem or challenge?
>
> What's not a problem in this?
>
> What do I really want to do?
>
> In What Ways Might I...
>
> How Might I ...
>
> How^2...

When it comes time to converge, the following questions will be useful:

> Which of the problem questions is the one for which ideas are most needed?
>
> Do some of these questions express similar concerns? What's the "common strand" among them? Can that be rephrased into a single problem question?
>
> Which of these questions suggest the most useful direction?
>
> What is really my most important concern?
>
> Where should I begin?
>
> Which of these captures the essence of my goals, objectives or wishes?

In Problem-Finding, the client chooses which of the possibilities best suits his/her needs. In bringing to bear criteria for choosing one of the problem questions, you may want to consult the chapter on Solution-Finding since it will have the fullest discussion of criteria for choosing among alternatives.

PROBLEM-FINDING

BEFORE YOU START: Make photocopies of the Problem-Finding Activities #1 through 4 (pages 47 -51) for each student. Distribute the activity sheets singly, as you become ready to use them.

Activity #1
To Get a Belt or be Belted
Suggestions for the Teacher:

Since this problem is stated as a problem that one person has, approach it as a "What would you do?" experience when it comes to converging. After students have opened up the possibilities for the statement of the problem, you could choose a student to "be" the client, and ask "If you were John, which of these problem statements would you want to use to get a lot of ideas for your use?" Another way of getting the students to converge is to say, "Which of these problem statements gets at the essence of the problem?" If you were John, which of these problem statements would give the main issue for you?"

What you want to end the session with is a working IWWMI statement that would be suitable for Idea-Finding, which is the next step.

Activity #2
The Mad Hatter
Suggestions for the Teacher:

This exercise has a lot of possibilities for alternate problem statements. As well, in converging to a single choice for Idea-Finding there will be an opportunity for the students to make use of criteria. Two such criteria might be: which is the most pressing, or which problem statement, if I come up with a workable solution, will take care of all or most of the others. When the students are converging, talk about what is going on so that they understand that the criterion they use makes a difference in what they end up selecting. You could use this exercise as an opportunity to show the conncection between choice of criterion and selection of alternative. For example, you could say to the students, if we use, "Which is the Problem Statement which will create the least social stir?" which one would you choose. Then you could say, which problem statement has the potential for the longest range of success (if we got it solved). Try others, using criteria from the chapter on Solution-Finding.

PROBLEM-FINDING

Activity #3
Family Friction
Suggestions for the Teacher:

46 This is a good activity to practice the "Why" process. In doing this, you ask yourself why this is a problem. The answer you get gives you one slant on the problem, which can usually be turned into a "How To" or an "In What Ways Might I"...problem question.

For example, in this problem I can imagine the following conversation with Sally.

Sally:	I've about had it with my family.
Friend:	Why is your family a problem?
Sally:	There is fighting all the time.
Friend:	So your problem could be "How To reduce fights."

Students can continue with this by asking "Why else?"

This activity works well as a small group activity. Be sure to leave time to get the whole group back together to share all the various ways of phrasing the problem. The converging, that is, the selection of the problem question to be used in Idea-Finding can be done as a whole group activity. In this one the class could vote or a volunteer could "be" Sally to make the choice. Ask the student who makes the choice what his/her criteria were for choosing. The teacher can get at that by asking, what was it that led you to choose that one.

Activity #4

Dealer's Choice
Suggestions for the Teacher:

Involving all the senses in CPS has been shown to be helpful. Use your imagination to think of ways to stimulate the student's thoughts as they work. This exercise could be done several times, choosing from the work in earlier exercises. If you've never facilitated CPS before, you might want to try one extra Problem-Finding stimulus instead of all three.

Stimulus suggestions:

Play a record for a couple minutes just before they write their first problem statement.

Pass around something that smells good as they begin redefining the problem.

Pass around photographs and pictures from magazines in the third round of expanding points of view.

In order for this to work in the usual class period time frame, advance preparation is essential. The smell stimulus could be drops of perfume on cotton balls. Have 10 prepared in advance. Have the pictures from magazines glued to background paper and ready to go. These pictures can be used several times. Assemble thirty, or at least one picture per student. The students can exchange the pictures.

After the students have selected the problem statement for Idea-Finding, take time to talk about the use of music, smell, and visual aids. Did the students get new ideas that way? What helped most?

PROBLEM-FINDING

Activity #1
TO GET A BELT OR BE BELTED

John, a seventh grader, came to his parents after six months of school and said, "Mom, Dad, I want to take Karate lessons. The only way to keep from being hassled at school is to be really tough. I'm pretty tough, but I'm no match for three or four guys when they gang up on me. I figure Karate is the answer." John's parents know that their son is dealing with a real problem. They know from first hand experience, incidents of violence at the school. They also know that students who make good grades are sometimes singled out as the "target" for harrassment or teasing. John is in the "top" group of students.

Before they sign their son up for Karate lessons the parents think that a further discussion of just what the problems <u>are</u> that John is facing would help.

Comment: Sometimes problems overlap. Sometimes there are sub-problems that have to be dealt with before you can handle the one that confronts you at first. In this instance John thinks his problem is that he's just not tough <u>enough</u> and Karate is the solution. However, there are a number of other factors that should be considered.

In Data-Finding with their son the following items were noted:

1) The harassment occurs when he's alone and in places where school personnel are absent.

2) The harassment is not always violent. It sometimes starts with teasing and John loses his temper, which then ends up in a fight.

3) The problem doesn't exist in the classes where John is with "His Group."

INSTRUCTIONS: Problem-Finding involves thinking over the mess, and redefining it.

In this exercise begin with: In what ways might John increase his ability to defend himself at school?

Now, restate this in as many ways as you can to get different ideas as to what the problem is.

Next, try looking at the problem from another point of view.

For example:

In what ways might the school administrators. . . a teacher. . . John's parents. . .

Finish these and add others.

PROBLEM-FINDING

TO GET A BELT OR BE BELTED continued

48   Try to get at least ten ways of stating John's problem.

_____

_____

_____

_____

_____

_____

_____

_____

Finish this exercise by selecting the statement that says it best for you.

_____

_____

_____

_____

PROBLEM-FINDING

Activity #2
THE MAD HATTER

Andrea was hired to paint flowers on hats at $2.50 a hat. Andrea is 18 and this is her first real money making job. She did the same thing last year. Andrea needs to make as much money as possible for college. There was some disagreement at first as to what she would be paid per hat since the woman who hired her had changed her position in the company after making the original non-written contract with Andrea. Nevertheless, Andrea was happy with the compromise of $2.50 per hat and a small commission on hats sold while she worked. The president of the company ordered 300 hats about halfway through the season and told her to go for it. Andrea began to paint flowers on hats, completing 20-30 a day. Suddenly, the woman who hired her and who also does some of the marketing, called to say that she may only paint as many as could be sold in the store where she was painting them. She was angry and yelling for no apparent reason. There were fourteen stores in the chain of stores. This company has a history of difficulty with the issue of "who has the final say." The main executives operate the business in an informal way with almost no written instructions passing among them. The business manager for the fourteen stores handles orders and distribution of soft goods, such as these hats. The manager of the store she works in is strongly supportive of Andrea and her work, as are the other staff members of the store. They are so supportive, in fact, that when Andrea told them about the message she got, they offered to walk off the job in protest if she wanted them to do that. The company depends on the income from the store Andrea works in, and at the height of the season such a threat or actual event would be very distressing to the company. The present store manager has increased the sales of the store dramatically. It is not a store where getting dependable management is easy.

When Andrea began to think about what to do, she first thought: In What Ways Might I get another source of income. Then she thought, In What Ways Might I increase the number of hats sold in this store.

Help Andrea out with Problem-Finding. Try to produce fifteen alternative ways of looking at her problem.

_____   _____
_____   _____
_____   _____
_____   _____
_____   _____
_____   _____
_____   _____

Now go back over the problem questions. If you were Andrea, which one would you choose for Idea-Finding? Why? Can you combine some and rephrase them to come up with one which will capture the most pressing concern?

PROBLEM-FINDING

Activity #3
FAMILY FRICTION

50 Sally says her family just isn't the all-American ideal she sees on television or reads about in magazines. She is really depressed and upset about it. When she reviewed some of the facts involved in her family life, the things that stood out in her mind included the following:

1. Sally (age 15) and Sam (age 13) don't get along, but it's not unbearable.

2. Sam and Steven (age 9) don't get along and it's really awful.

3. The personalities in her family are quite different, but each in his/her own way is very strong and dominant, except the youngest.

4. There doesn't seem to be anything that everyone in the family enjoys doing together. "Family" outings aren't very successful.

5. Sally's parents seem really committed to "family" outings.

When Sally finished Data-Finding, she stated her first view of the mess as:

In What Ways Might I improve my family life..

Then she rephrased it to:

In What Ways Might I reduce the tension between my brothers..

Now it's time for you to see how many ways you can phrase the problem. Aim for ten new ways of stating the problem. Try to get the quota in fifteen minutes.

Some suggestions:

See what happens when you change the verbs in the problem.

See what happens when you focus on different people in the problem.

What happens when you close your eyes and dream up a completely new way of looking at the problem?

PROBLEM-FINDING

Activity #4
DEALER'S CHOICE

Now that you've had some experience with Problem-Finding, take one of the problems from the first section of the book. Use that problem to complete this Problem-Finding exercise. You might try "Personal Inventory," or "Boredom in the Classroom," or one from "Challenges for the 21st Century." Using a real problem gives the best results in the long run. Remember to save the work.

Reviewing the steps so far:

You've got a mess or problem situation to solve or do something about. Perhaps you 've got something to improve.

You've asked yourself the Data-Finding questions such as:

Who is involved?
Why is this important?
What do I hope to gain?
Why is this a problem?
What possible causes do I know about?
What are my goals in this?
What has been done already to solve this?

You've marked the most important data.

Now, write out your first problem statement: In What Ways Might I...

_____

Next: Redefine your statement: List four new ways of stating the problem.

_____   _____

_____   _____

Then: Change the point of view and restate the problem again.

_____

Look again at the answers to the Data-Finding questions. Write out some problem questions based on those answers.

_____

_____

Finish by selecting the problem question that best expresses your present needs/wishes. Maybe one of the statements jumps out at you. Perhaps one stands head and shoulders above the rest. If so, your choice is easy.

PROBLEM-FINDING

Introduction To Idea-Finding

All of the suggestions in the first chapter apply to Idea-Finding. By now your students have had some practice in the freewheeling atmosphere of brainstorming. Remember that wild, silly, fantastic ideas can form the basis for highly innovative solutions to problems which are then modified to meet the demands of the client.

Another technique which can be useful in stimulating ideas is that of forced relationships. In this technique, the principle of an analogy is used, but the similarity between the two situations is not obvious, thus the term "forced." In practice, the facilitator might suggest a forced relationship at some point in Idea-Finding when the flow has stopped. For example, in Problem-Finding, the students came up with a number of different ways of looking at the Family Friction situation. Let's suppose that the problem statement chosen was In What Ways Might We improve family outings? Now, let's suppose that a number of ideas have been suggested and the group is at a plateau. The leader says, "What ideas does the world of gardening and agriculture trigger for this problem?"

The task then is to think of the connections that can be made. A student might say, "Well, in agriculture they rotate their crops. Maybe the family outings could be rotated with each family member taking turns on deciding what's to be done." In facilitating, the leader chooses a realm that is removed from the problem area to insure a new slant.

To keep the perspective accurate, there are many Idea-Finding sessions where no special prompting is necessary. The suggestions in chapter one and here are aimed at those times when ideas begin to slow down.

The following list of questions may prove useful in Idea-Finding sessions.

> What are some options?
> What's a new way to handle this situation?
> If I had a magic wand how would I solve this problem?
> What fantasy solutions can you offer?
> What analogies might help?
> Think of the opposite situation. Does that suggest an idea?
> Take a wild dream and visualize a solution.
> How might some objects from a totally different area suggest a solution?
> What new connections can be made?

IDEA-FINDING

After a brainstorming session there may be a wall covered with large newsprint pages filled with suggestions. Narrowing down the array to the most promising possibilities is next. The following questions will be helpful in converging at the end of Idea-Finding.

> Are there some that stand head and shoulders above the rest?
> What ideas caught my attention?
> Can some of the ideas go together?
> Which ideas offer you the best chance to do something?
> If I could make them work, which would I like?
> Which ones are the most appealing?

How far you converge will depend on how many ideas have been generated. After Idea-Finding, choosing between 6-12 of the most promising ideas will put you in a comfortable spot to start Solution-Finding. This chapter will suggest various strategies for reducing the list of ideas to a managable number.

IDEA-FINDING

BEFORE YOU START: Make photocopies of the Idea-Finding Activities #1 through 5 (pages 57 - 61) for each student. Distribute the activity sheets singly, as you become ready to use them.

Activity #1
Laughter Unlimited
Suggestions for the Teacher:

This activity is a good one for group work. Have a student with a good, clear handwriting record the ideas. Number the ideas as they come. The class could also work in two groups with the newsprint taped or tacked at opposite ends. After the general brainstorming, join the groups and the sheets of ideas. Have someone read all the ideas and then go to the convergent activities.

Activity #2
Sock Matching
Suggestions for the Teacher:

In the classroom, this activity has been greeted with a great deal of enthusiasm. It wouldn't be surprising if one of the ideas generated from the session found its way into the market place. It has worked well both as a large group activity and in small groups. If you choose small groups, be sure to leave time at the end to share the work done.

Activity #3
The Chocolate Bunny Caper
Suggestions for the Teacher:

This exercise will give the student a chance to think of some creative uses for household objects. The problem situation was an authentic one. It took the children involved an hour to solve.

In a situation like this, Solution-Finding becomes very simple. Find an idea that works without destroying the candy.

The exercise works well in small groups or as a total class. Piggybacking on ideas and hitchhiking is common.

Activity #4
Five Grand
Suggestions for the Teacher:

FIRST BRAINSTORMING: Sometimes students think automatically and almost exclusively of *buying* this or that when extra money comes along. The first brainstorming should stretch the thinking of the students to include a variety of uses.

IDEA-FINDING

Ask the students to list in columns all the verbs they can think of that would suggest different sorts of <u>uses</u> for the money. Have them group the verbs that mean about the same thing together, so that you end up with several groups or words divided into categories across their paper.

Example: Buy:

purchase: (other verbs)

spend it on getting:

acquire

After they've made their first list of verbs, ask them to think of opposites to those words. To those suggest *new* ways of using the money. Write them down in a separate column.

SECOND BRAINSTORMING: Have the students fill in their ideas down the columns using the various mind jogging suggestions mentioned in previous sections. You could use smells, music, word association, etc.

THIRD BRAINSTORMING: Group the students in threes. Let them line their papers up together so they can see what's there. Ask them to make combinations, to substitute some of the action words from one column to one or two of the other columns to get new ideas. After each suggestion, have them write down the new ideas.

FINISHING UP: Complete the session with a master list on a large sheet of paper, so that all the students can see the results. This can be done by having students come up and share what they have, adding only the new ideas as they come. By using a paper instead of the chalkboard, you won't have to re-copy the list. Save the list for the activity in Solution-Finding.

Converging

In this exercise there is often a very large number of ideas that is generated. Using highlighting to narrow down the choices for Solution-Finding in such an exercise works well. In highlighting, the client (in this case it will be individual students) looks over the list and circles the ideas which pop out at him/her for whatever reason. The student is not to worry, at this point, whether they are able to make it happen. In a list of fifty items, students may circle 10-15 items that strike them as appealing or intriguing. The next step is to group together those "hits" that have something in common. The student should be explicit about what the "hits" have in common. The "hits" are then "hot spots." Suppose the list of fifty ideas can be reduced to fifteen "hits" and those "hits" can be further grouped into five "hot spots." The last task before the student goes into thorough Solution-Finding is to rephrase what the "hot spots" represent to the student. At this point the student/client will have five options which have strong appeal from which to choose.

IDEA-FINDING

56 This technique for converging is appropriate when there are a number of very appealing ideas, none of which, leaps out as a clear "winner" to the client.

It is very likely that this activity will take more than a single class period. The natural division point is to complete brainstorming in one session and then to start the next class period with converging.

Activity #5
Dealer's Choice
Suggestions for the Teacher:

By the time the class has gotten to this stage there is rarely a lack of possibilities to choose among. Any of the previous Problem-Finding exercises could be used, however, at this point it is a good idea to get an authentic issue from the students. The book has provided situations that have almost all come from real life, but nothing can compare to working with problems and challenges chosen by the students.

The most important thing to remember at this stage is that if you choose a real issue, you need to be prepared to follow through with Solution- Finding and Acceptance-Finding. A personal story illustrates what is meant. Some years ago I heard a fairly well known man reporting how he had used problem solving with students. They had decided to do something about the rude way the cafeteria help had been treating the students as they went through the lunch line. The students had generated a number of ideas and had settled on having the principal talk to the workers. They were disappointed with the results. As a matter of fact, the workers seemed less pleasant than before. When questioned about the stage of Acceptance-Finding, he confessed to having used a short form of CPS. What you do with your solution ideas, how you refine them, and prepare the way for getting them accepted is an extremely important part of CPS and can often make the difference between success and failure.

Activity #1
LAUGHTER UNLIMITED

Laura and Scott have just found themselves in a real predicament. They are part of a spe-
cially selected team, and represent their school. Their team has won an award and along
with representatives from teams all over the country, they are seated on a platform in front
of a large crowd. There is a well respected, nationally known person speaking. This person
is giving the history of the competition that their school has just won. The awards will be
presented shortly. Suddenly, Laura and Scott are seized with a desire to laugh. Their bodies
are beginning to shake...

In What Ways Might They Keep From Laughing?

_____

_____

_____

_____

_____

_____

_____

_____

_____

_____

_____

Converging on a choice:

Since the time element is an obvious factor here, which of the choices can be implemented
the quickest?

_____

_____

_____

Which of the ideas offer the best chance of being effective:

_____

Which of the ideas can be combined to provide a more powerful solution?

_____

_____

IDEA-FINDING

Activity #2
SOCK MATCHING

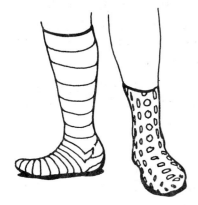

Here's a challenge that might make you some money. Have you ever had trouble finding socks that match? After the family wash is done, are there "leftover" socks? Have you ever calculated the work hours in a year that a large family might spend just matching socks?

Here's your challenge: How many ideas can you come up with to solve this problem? Choose one, two or three of the following problem statements to generate ideas — depending on the time available. Remember: In Idea Finding you don't <u>judge</u> the ideas — that comes afterwards. Here, what you want is as <u>many</u> ideas as possible.

1. In what ways might I eliminate lost socks...
2. In what ways might we reduce sock matching time...
3. In what ways might one eliminate the need to match socks...
4. In what ways might I eliminate lost socks and reduce sock matching time simultaneously...

If you get interested in follow-up, write to the U.S. Patent Office for information on how to patent an idea.

Converging

Which of the ideas will get the job done?

_____

Choose one for further development. List three strengths, or advantages. Next list three potentials, or future gains. Finish with three concerns, areas for further improvement.

_____
_____
_____
_____
_____
_____
_____
_____

IDEA-FINDING

Activity #3

THE CHOCOLATE BUNNY CAPER

The annual candy hunt at the Lawrence house had always been a high point of the year. With each passing year the candy was hidden in harder and harder places. Just the hiding of the candy became quite a challenge for the parents.

Mrs. Lawrence knew one last really hard place that she'd been "saving." What she didn't know was that this place was to become a real <u>problem</u> or from another point of view—"quite a challenge."

This is what happened in the Lawrence household. The night before the big candy hunt Mrs. Lawrence removed the 100 year old loose piece of wood from its position at the top of the book case column and set the chocolate bunny in its carton in the empty space on top of the insulation and replaced the wood.

The next morning after a lengthy search, the hiding place was gleefully discovered. However, the cheers turned to "Oh, No!" as the children watched the chocolate bunny slowly disappear from view atop a "bed" of insulation. To understand their dilemma you will find a picture of where the candy came to rest on page 60.

In what ways might the children retrieve the chocolate bunny?

_____

_____

_____

_____

_____

_____

_____

_____

_____

_____

_____

_____

_____

_____

_____

_____

_____

IDEA-FINDING

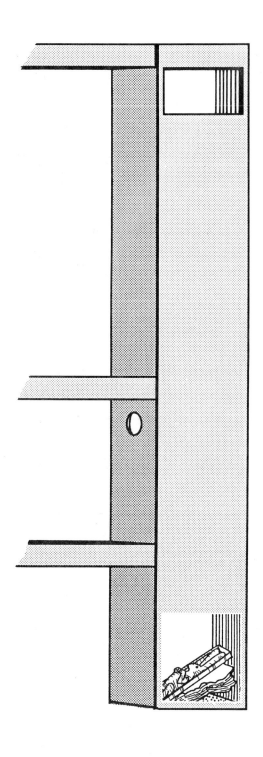

Scale: 1 inch to 1 foot

Solid board above

5" opening: "the chute" the bunny went down

Wood: 1 1/2" thick

The "chute" is mostly empty

The loose board has been removed

7 feet from bottom to top of bookcase

Knothole 2" in diameter, 3 feet from the floor

Very sturdy walnut one-piece board 1 1/2" thick

Chocolate bunny at bottom - 8 oz. solid chocolate in paper & plastic wrapped carton resting on some fluffy fiberglass insulation. Box is 4" x 6".

IDEA-FINDING

Activity #4
FIVE GRAND

You've just won $5,000.00 in a give away contest. You actually have $5,000.00 to use as you wish.
Taxes on the money have already been paid.

In what ways might you use $5,000.00? (Save your list for the next activity)

_____
_____
_____
_____
_____
_____
_____
_____
_____
_____
_____
_____
_____
_____
_____
_____
_____
_____
_____

Activity #5
DEALER'S CHIOICE

Here's your chance to get some help from an effective resource team. By now your classmates have become expert at generating ideas. What better way to get some new ideas on a
problem that's been bugging you. All you have to do is share your problem statement.

If this is a problem which hasn't been done in class up to this point, some time will be
needed to share the Data-Finding and Problem-Finding stages. If you are a client, be con-
cise, give your resource group the most important facts about the problem and give them a
clear focus for Idea-Finding.

In What Ways Might I...

IDEA-FINDING

Introduction To Solution - Finding

In Creative Problem Solving, Solution-Finding is the place for deciding which idea or ideas to use in solving your problem. Whether you decide to choose on the basis of "chance" as in flipping a coin, or on the basis of the idea that's the least expensive, or a combination of several, still you have to decide.

There are a lot of different ways to go about evaluating ideas. This portion of the book is designed to help prepare you for making good judgments and refining ideas.

Many Ideas

CONVERGENCE TAKES PLACE

Solution Choice

When you choose some ideas from a list, you're making decisions, but the other ideas need not be <u>discarded</u>. They may be used <u>later</u>, they may trigger still other ideas or they may be combined as part of the solution for the problem.

Making Judgments and Evaluating

Many teenagers don't want to make judgments. "To each his own," "One person's opinion is as good as another," "It's all a matter of opinion," are phrases frequently heard. Certainly our society is more open now to being easy about a variety of opinions than it was 100 years ago. Still, beyond matters of personal preference, there lies a lot of territory where sound judgment is needed. Developing that ability takes time.

There are several strategies for selecting among the alternatives which Idea-Finding has produced. At the end of Idea-Finding the convergent part will have narrowed down the large number of ideas to those that have the most promise.

This chapter introduces several of the Solution-Finding strategies. In addition to those strategies, there are two preparation exercises for teenagers which deal with using criteria as a separate issue.

Before actual Solution-Finding can begin, the client must decide on what criteria will be used. The following questions are given as an aid in getting that information.

SOLUTION-FINDING

What criteria might be considered?
What "yardsticks" might we use in judging these ideas?
How might we assess the strengths and weakness of these ideas?
What factors should we consider if we are going to develop, or improve these ideas?
How can the most interesting ideas be made stronger or better?
How can we make some of the fantasy ideas more practical and realistic?
What makes some of the ideas less interesting?
What are the appealing features among the ideas? How can we combine these features?

These Kind of Questions	Suggest These Criteria
1. Is the cost to follow this solution too great for present resources?	Cost
2. How long will it take to use this solution?	Time
3. Would someone get hurt doing this?	Safety
4. Is it a short-term solution, or will you have to solve the problem again soon?	Durability
5. Is the idea for the solution repulsive?	Aesthetics
6. In carrying out this idea for the solution, would a law be broken?	Legality
7. Is the action proposed within our power?	Realistic
8. What is the probability that the results which are hoped for - will indeed be brought about by this course of action? Will it work?	Likelihood for success
9. What will we have to give up or sacrifice to carry out this idea?	Extent of sacrifice
10. Is the sacrifice involved worth it?	Worth the sacrifice
11. What other effects, other than the hoped for effects, are likely to result if we carry out this solution idea — And are those effects desirable?	Value of other effects
12. Is the solution idea moral? Would acting on this idea require lying, cheating, abusing?	Morality
13. Can this solution idea be combined with others to increase likelihood of success?	Combination
14. Is this a solution idea which, if you don't do it, or parts of it, the problem won't get solved?	Bottom line
15. Does this solution fit into the present way of doing things?	Risk

SOLUTION-FINDING

After the possible yardsticks are chosen, the student must select a few to use in a given problem. Which criteria are chosen will vary with the nature of the problem. In this section a long list of possibilities is given in order to make your resources complete. It will be important, however, not to overpower or flood your class with too much at once. The following questions will be helpful in choosing among criteria.

What criteria are the most important to me?
Which of these are essential?
Which of these various means of judging will best help us refine and develop ideas?

SOLUTION-FINDING

BEFORE YOU START: Make photocopies of the Solution-Finding Activities #1 through 4 (pages 67-73) for each student. Distribute the activity sheets singly, as you become ready to use them.

Activity #1
A Perfect Pen
Suggestions for the Teacher:

Prior Preparation:

Taking the time to gather some really awful pens will be worth the effort. Good pens can perhaps come from the class. To be safe, bring one or two good pens.

Activity #2
Doomsday Plus 10 and Counting
Suggestions for the Teacher:

Divide the class into groups of convenient size. You can use the same topic for several groups. Groups that have more than four often don't work well.

<u>Goal:</u> The goal for this activity is to enable students to see that which criteria are used in evaluating a course of action can make an important difference in the outcome. It is a preparation for sorting through the various solutions that come up in Creative Problem Solving.

Activity #3
Sifting and Sorting the Solutions
Suggestions for the Teacher:

The Solution-Finding Matrix which accompanies this exercise may be used several times. Use it with any of the earlier problems which have generated a large number of solutions. It can be used as an alternative to the converging activities at the end of Idea-Finding. The advantage of using it is that students are forced to be explicit about their criteria for choosing. One disadvantage is that it takes a fair amount of time.

Your judgment as facilitator is needed as you decide which form of converging to use with Idea-Finding. If there seems to be one very compelling idea which the client wants to develop, then using the PPC (Pluses, Potential, & Concerns) which is introduced next would be more appropriate.

SOLUTION-FINDING

Activity #4

Hot Air Ballooning

Suggestions for the Teacher:

This activity gives students a chance to practice a very practical method of Solution-Finding. PPC stands for Plusses, Potentials, and Concerns. This activity will get students to take an idea and work with it to note the strengths, look at future gains or spin offs and then list three possible concerns someone may have. After this is done, students rework the solution to improve the original idea such that the concerns are taken care of in the final plan. In the excitement of a "great idea," students sometimes want to "run with it" before the concerns are considered. This exercise gives them a chance to see how you can work with an idea to improve it.

Activity #1
A PERFECT PEN

Suppose you were about to put on the market a new line of pens. Since you know personal taste varies, you plan to have a variety of types, ball point, acrylic tip, as well as a cartridge type to hold ink, plus various sized points to suit individual preferences. You have a terrific group on your staff to make those decisions for you. What you're concerned with is the <u>basic</u> question. What makes any pen a <u>good</u> pen for any user?

A basic property is one that won't vary from person to person. For example, one basic property of a good pen is producing a <u>continuous</u> line. A matter of taste, on the other hand would be the color of the pen.

TASK I: Divide the class into 3 parts. Appoint someone to be recorder in each.

> **Group One:** List all the things you can think of that would make a pen an <u>awful</u> pen. Don't include things that are a matter of personal taste. Suggestion: Pretend you are going to devise the world's worst pen, what would you include?

> **Group Two:** List all the characteristics that make up a really <u>good</u> pen.

> **Group Three:** Examine the pens. What is there about the good ones that make them better than the "junkers." Make a list of these characteristics. Keep your list limited to basic characteristics, not things like color or decorations choice. After you've had a chance to examine the pens, give them to the other groups for examination.

TASK II: Make a master list of the criteria (standards) you have developed for rating pens that don't depend on matters of individual preference.

TASK III: Prepare a Pen Rating Matrix and rate some pens in the class.

SOLUTION-FINDING

A PERFECT PEN continued

Pen Rating Sheet

Enter Criteria:

PENS:

A. _____

B. _____

C. _____

D. _____

E. _____

Use this scale for each criterion, as you rate each pen:
4 = satisfies the criterion completely
2 or 3 = satisfy criteria partially
1 = does not satisfy the criteria at all

SOLUTION-FINDING

Activity #2
DOOMSDAY PLUS 10 AND COUNTING

Your social studies class has been given an exercise in values clarification. There is only one small town left on earth. There are 700 people. It was situated outside a large city and many people commuted to work. The population is a mixture of just about every sort of person from the destroyed society. Fifteen people can be saved from these last 700. Your teacher is very interested in the <u>basis</u> on which the decision is made, not the mechanics. This activity is designed to help you see that the criteria (the basis for judging) you use make a great difference in the outcome.

Circle the group description that describes the group you are in.

GROUP #1: Criterion #1 — Utility For Restoring the Lost Society

Fifteen people will be chosen who will be most useful in replacing the destroyed society. What characteristics, abilities, etc. would be the ones to look for? How could those people be selected?

GROUP #2: Criterion #2 — Justice or Fairness

Criterion is based on the belief that human life is equally precious. Describe as many ways as you can by which a fair selection among the 700 people could be made.

GROUP #3: Suppose it was decided that simply "replacing the old society" was not the goal, instead the goal would be to aim at the "best society that can be realistically hoped for."

List the qualities, characteristics, and abilities that you would look for in the persons who would build the society.

SOLUTION-FINDING

SIFTING AND SORTING THE SOLUTIONS

70 In this activity you will use either the list of ideas which you generated for how to spend $5,000.00 or the list provided. If you use your own list start this exercise with the entire list before you begin converging. The Solution-Finding Matrix provides a slightly more formal way of converging than the one suggested in Idea-Finding. Knowing how to use both methods can be helpful.

Instructions:

FIRST: Your first task is to reduce the list of ideas from seventy to no more than thirty-nine. A simple way to do this is to begin listing the ways that have some appeal and eliminate those that don't. If you don't have as many as thirty-nine that's o.k. too.

SECOND: After you have the most promising listed next to a number, then select your criteria from those listed in the introduction to this chapter (your teacher can photocopy a list for you), or put in your own criteria. Note: If you don't want to spend your money all at once, make that one of your criteria..namely "won't use it all at once."

THIRD: Judge the ideas on the listed criteria. Do they stay in for further consideration, or are they out for now?

FOURTH: When you're finished, see which ones are in on each of the criteria. You will probably have the list reduced quite a bit.

IDEAS FOR USING $5,000.00
These were constructed by a group of high school students in York, New York.

BUY:
clothes
car
swimming pool
tools
stereo equipment
condominium
clock
motor bike
shoes
class ring
a cat
antiques
chocolate
a unicorn
art materials
books
sports equipment
hang glider
volleyball
piano
furniture

INVEST:
in stocks
bonds
money market
business ventures
art studio
herb garden/factory
a cat farm
art work
a movie
in materials for black magic —
    becoming a practicing witch

SAVE:
for college
in a savings account
savings bonds

INSULATE:
house with $1,000.00 bills

SLEEP:
on it — as in a mattress

PUBLISH:
a book on poetry

RENT:
apartment
a music hall
cottage on the lake

LEND:
to needy persons

SPEND ON:
travel to: South America,
Canada, Greece, cross country
summer camp
lessons in art
redecorating
entertainment: ballet, movies,
    food, parties
downpayment on house

BURN:
the money

SOLUTION-FINDING

Solution Finding Matrix-
When the Solutions are Numerous

Problem: IWWMI   CRITERIA   71

_____

Solution Ideas	in	out	in	out	in	out	in	out	in	out	in	out
1. _____												
2. _____												
3. _____												
4. _____												
5. _____												
6. _____												
7. _____												
8. _____												
9. _____												
10. _____												
11. _____												
12. _____												
13. _____												
14. _____												
15. _____												
16. _____												
17. _____												
18. _____												
19. _____												
20. _____												
21. _____												
22. _____												
23. _____												
24. _____												
25. _____												
26. _____												
27. _____												
28. _____												
29. _____												
30. _____												
31. _____												
32. _____												
33. _____												
34. _____												
35. _____												
36. _____												
37. _____												
38. _____												
39. _____												
40. _____												

SOLUTION-FINDING

Activity #4
HOT AIR BALLOONING

72   For years Georgia had wanted to write the film script for an exciting movie which featured hot air ballooning. This was no wild eyed wish. Georgia owned her own hot air balloon company and was an expert pilot, not just of balloons, but of airplanes. During the summer she worked for a plush resort giving rides to the clients of the hotel. The resort was set in the midst of magnificient scenery. During a problem solving session, one of the ideas that was offered struck Georgia with force. The idea was to film part of the movie during the upcoming hot air ballooning event. Hot air balloonists would be coming to the resort from all over the country and their presence would provide tremendous visual opportunities for the movie. She has about six months to plan what happens. At this point the use of PPC looks good to the problem solving facilitator.

Instructions:

Imagine the quiet, plush resort and the big hot air ballooning event with extra people, equipment and needs. Imagine the film company and its equipment. Now, in the space below list three pluses (strengths, useful aspects, or advantages) to the proposed solution to use the balloon event for part of the movie filming.

_____

_____

_____

Next:
List three potential positive spin-offs from this plan. What future gains could the plan produce?

_____

_____

_____

Next:
List three possible concerns someone might have about the solution idea.

_____

_____

_____

SOLUTION-FINDING

Finally:

Go back over the concerns and come up with ways that the strengths or potential spin-off ideas can be used to overcome the concerns. Or rephrase the solution idea to overcome the concerns, changing the direction of the solution idea. At this point the original solution idea will get modified to make the solution idea stronger and more acceptable.

_____

_____

_____

_____

_____

_____

_____

_____

_____

_____

_____

_____

_____

_____

_____

_____

_____

_____

_____

_____

_____

_____

SOLUTION-FINDING

Introduction to Acceptance-Finding

74 Many good ideas have failed because Acceptance-Finding was skipped or not undertaken thoroughly and honestly.

Sometimes good ideas never get put into practice because the person with the idea failed to prepare the way for the idea to get accepted. It is a well-known fact that people don't like change. Getting ready for change helps.

In this phase of Creative Problem Solving, students are introduced to a variety of techniques which will help new ideas get a "warm welcome." Teachers will find many applications for the techniques discussed here.

When changing something, looking for potential trouble spots and sources of help and assistance ahead of time really makes a difference. This is part of the task of Acceptance - Finding. Possible trouble or resistance is identified and appropriate responses are formulated. Planning how to use your "Assisters" or support people to prevent trouble before it starts is also part of Acceptance-Finding.

Then, a plan to implement the ideas needs to be formulated. This is the major goal of Acceptance-Finding. There are specific steps to follow. At the end of Acceptance-Finding, there should be a clear idea of what should be done in the next 24 hours, the next few weeks, as well as a long range action plan. Agreement must be reached as to who will take the responsibility for checking or enacting each part of the action plan.

ACCEPTANCE-FINDING

BEFORE YOU START: Make photocopies of the Accepting-Finding Activities #1 through 3 (pages 76 to 81) for each student. Distribute the activity sheets singly, as you become ready to use them.

Activity #1
Contention in the Cafeteria (Part I)
Suggestions for the Teacher:

This exercise makes use of an actual problem solving situation. To help insure success, students are given instructions for Acceptance-Finding. The situation is one many people have encountered, so detailed preparation will probably not be necessary.

Divide your class into small groups and have each group choose a preferred solution (either A or B). The first part of the exercise should take about half the class period. There are two parts to Activity #1: First, getting some general ideas about getting the chosen solution accepted. Second, getting specific data for Acceptance-Finding. There are two Acceptance-Finding Data Sheets. After entering the data, half of the class time should be used to summarize what has been learned about the task at hand. Each group could report their findings. It is possible that the work of the groups lends itself to combining and changing the two solutions into one more powerful one. If so, be open to that and help the class see how the suggested data can be combined into a single more powerful plan. The last part of Acceptance-Finding is described in Activity #2 and Activity #3 and should be considered as a unit. Divide the exercises to suit your own schedule and time frame. At the end of these three exercises, your students will have a grasp of how to plan specific action steps. These steps are the same for most any problem they choose to tackle.

Activity #2
Contention in the Cafeteria (Part II)
Suggestions for the Teacher:

This activity is based on Activity #1 and the ACCEPTANCE-FINDING DATA SHEETS. In Activity #1 there were two solutions which were chosen for final use and Acceptance-Finding was done on both ideas. At this point, the class may have thought of ways to improve and combine those two ideas. Or, separate action plans may be emerging. Use your judgment about how to proceed. Use Activity #2 to get specific commitments for the action plan.

Activity #3
Contention in the Cafeteria (Part III)
Suggestions for the Teacher:

This activity is designed to give the students a sense of long range planning. Such planning helps insure success. The "Lunchroom Courtesy Campaign" willl serve to illustrate this. The students may need some help constructing their time line. In general, this takes the information from the data sheets, which has now been roughly put in order on Activity #2 and puts it all into a time line for a long range plan. It should result in things that need to get done (naming groups, etc.) in various months.

ACCEPTANCE-FINDING

Activity #1
CONTENTION IN THE CAFETERIA Part I

WHO   WHY   WHAT   WHEN   WHERE   HOW

It is November. A group of sixth graders has been unhappy about the rudeness of the cafeteria staff for some time. In talking with each other, they decided it was a problem they wanted to do something about. After discussion, their selected solutions included:

A) Have a talk with the staff about the problem of rudeness.

B) Begin a "Lunchroom Courtesy Campaign" that would include everyone in an effort to improve, not just single out the cafeteria staff.

INSTRUCTIONS: Divide into several groups. Have 2 or 3 groups working on the same topic. Circle which solution your group is working on. To help assure success for a solution idea you need to think about the difficulties that may come up, how you can modify your ideas to be accepted. The time to do that is before you begin to carry out your idea.

First: Write down <u>any</u> thoughts that you have concerning getting this idea to work, getting it accepted. What do you anticipate happening? How can you get maximum acceptance?

Next: Fill in the <u>Acceptance-Finding Data Sheet.</u>

ACCEPTANCE-FINDING

Activity #1
CONTENTION IN THE CAFETERIA Part I

ACCEPTANCE-FINDING DATA SHEET - PART I: ASSISTERS

WHO   might help with this idea? List groups and individuals.

_____

_____

_____

_____

WHERE   is the weakest spot in this solution idea?

_____

_____

_____

_____

WHAT   can we do to strengthen the weak spots?

_____

_____

_____

_____

WHY   might someone want to help with this?

_____

_____

_____

_____

WHY   would someone not want to help make this work?

_____

_____

_____

_____

ACCEPTANCE-FINDING

CONTENTION IN THE CAFETERIA Part I continued

WHAT   can I do to convince someone to help?

_____

_____

_____

_____

WHAT   will be my biggest obstacles in carrying out this idea?

_____

_____

_____

_____

HOW   can I overcome these obstacles?

_____

_____

_____

_____

WHAT   needs to be done <u>before</u> we begin to carry out this idea?

_____

_____

_____

_____

WHAT   are some action plans for this idea? Do we need more?

_____

_____

_____

WHEN   is the best time to ask someone to help with this idea?

_____

_____

_____

_____

ACCEPTANCE-FINDING

Activity #2
CONTENTION IN THE CAFETERIA Part II

INSTRUCTIONS: Working out a time line as well as chart for who has responsibility for different aspects to the action plan can avoid misunderstanding and trouble. Take the time now to do that.

Use the two solution ideas from Activity #1 as well as the data sheets for Acceptance-Finding. With that information, complete this activity.

Who will take responsibility for action today?

_____

_____

What will they do?

_____

_____

What should happen next?

_____

_____

Then what?

_____

_____

What is your target date for successful completion of this?

_____

_____

Sometimes it helps to set up target dates for intermediate goals:

By date _____ , person _____ , will have _____

_____

_____

ACCEPTANCE-FINDING

Activity #3
CONTENTION IN THE CAFETERIA Part III

80 Use the Acceptance-Finding plans for "Lunchroom Courtesy Campaign" to construct a time line for action. The school year gives natural markers to use. Create a time line using deadlines that make sense. What would you want to happen each month or every two months? Consult your data sheets for specific details. Put in who will check on progress and how that will be done.

SEPTEMBER _____

_____

_____

_____

_____

OCTOBER _____

_____

_____

_____

NOVEMBER _____

_____

_____

_____

DECEMBER _____

_____

_____

_____

JANUARY _____

_____

_____

_____

ACCEPTANCE-FINDING

Activity #3
CONTENTION IN THE CAFETERIA Part III continued

FEBRUARY _____
        _____
        _____
        _____
        _____

MARCH   _____
        _____
        _____
        _____
        _____

APRIL   _____
        _____
        _____
        _____
        _____

MAY   _____
        _____
        _____
        _____
        _____

JUNE   _____
        _____
        _____
        _____
        _____

Describe what you will consider your signs of success.

_____
_____
_____

ACCEPTANCE-FINDING

Getting Your Act Together

Suggestions for the Teacher:

At this point in the course, you need to get the students to "put it all together." Be open to suggestions from the students. They may have several "real world" problems they would like to tackle by now. Help them do it!

One of the difficulties that may have come up using this textbook is that the steps in the process were isolated. At this point the students need to get acquainted with the flow of the whole step-by-step way of CPS.

"Graffiti Center" has been included for this purpose. This would be appropriate for a group. Be sure to include an individual problem solving opportunity as well.

GETTING YOUR

Activity #1
GRAFFITI CENTER

Graffiti in inappropriate places has been a plague for public buildings for years. Many solutions have been suggested with varying degrees of success. One idea that has "caught on" all over the world is to designate a particular place as the "Graffiti Center." This gives a place for expression and has apparently reduced the incidence of "inappropriate graffiti."

Consider yourself a part of a group who has been given permission to set up such a spot. The "Graffiti Center" at present is an 8 foot high and 50 foot long wooden fence that partially protects passersby from a baseball field adjacent to school property. The committee wants to encourage <u>creative</u>, non obscene graffiti. Your group can use the fence as long as the area remains clean and the fence doesn't become filled with obscene remarks.

Your initial problem statement is:

"In what ways might we encourage creative, non obscene graffiti at the Graffiti Center?"

As you complete the steps, fill in the squares.

ACT TOGETHER

CREATIVE PROBLEM SOLVING

Three Main Components
and Six Specific Stages

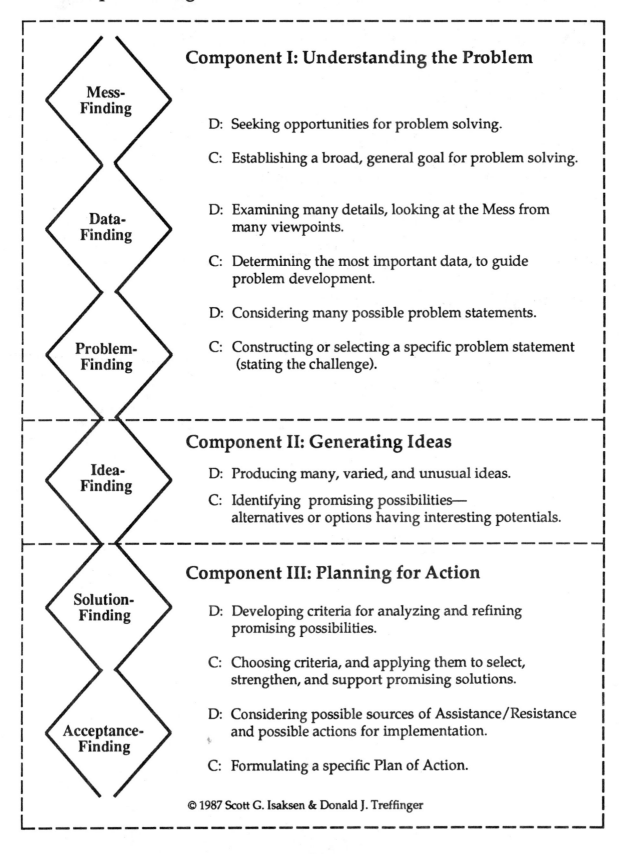

Component I: Understanding the Problem

Mess-Finding

D: Seeking opportunities for problem solving.

C: Establishing a broad, general goal for problem solving.

Data-Finding

D: Examining many details, looking at the Mess from many viewpoints.

C: Determining the most important data, to guide problem development.

Problem-Finding

D: Considering many possible problem statements.

C: Constructing or selecting a specific problem statement (stating the challenge).

Component II: Generating Ideas

Idea-Finding

D: Producing many, varied, and unusual ideas.

C: Identifying promising possibilities—alternatives or options having interesting potentials.

Component III: Planning for Action

Solution-Finding

D: Developing criteria for analyzing and refining promising possibilities.

C: Choosing criteria, and applying them to select, strengthen, and support promising solutions.

Acceptance-Finding

D: Considering possible sources of Assistance/Resistance and possible actions for implementation.

C: Formulating a specific Plan of Action.

© 1987 Scott G. Isaksen & Donald J. Treffinger